THE IROQUOIS

A First Americans Book

Virginia Driving Hawk Sneve

illustrated by Ronald Himler

Holiday House/New York

ACKNOWLEDGMENTS

The following selections are taken from *Songs from This Earth on Turtle's Back: Contemporary American Indian Poetry*, Joseph Bruchac, ed. (Greenfield Center, NY: The Greenfield Review Press, 1983): Peter Blue Cloud's (Mohawk) quotation is from his poem "Elderberry Flute Song"; Maurice Kenny's (Mohawk) quotations are from his poem "They Tell Me I Am Lost," and his essay "Spawnings" (last copyright © 1987 by Maurice Kenny, *Between Two Rivers: Selected Poems,* White Pine Press); Beth Brant's (Mohawk) quotations are from her essay "Native Origin," and her poem "Ride the Turtle's Back"; Roberta Hill Whiteman's (Oneida) quotation is from her poem "In the Longhouse, Oneida Museum."

The Peacemaker, Thanksgiving Address, and Knowledge of the Elders selections are from *Knowledge of the Elders,* José Barreiro and Carol Cornelius, eds., Akwe: Kon Press, Cornell University, 1991.

Library of Congress Cataloging-in-Publication Data
Sneve, Virginia Driving Hawk.
The Iroquois / by Virginia Driving Hawk Sneve ; illustrated by
Ronald Himler. — 1st ed.
p.   cm. — (A First Americans book)
Includes bibliographical references and index.
ISBN 0-8234-1163-X
1. Iroquois Indians — Juvenile literature. [1. Iroquois Indians.
2. Indians of North America.] I. Himler, Ronald, ill. II. Title.
III. Series: Sneve, Virginia Driving Hawk. First Americans book.
E99.I7S625   1995   94-3748   CIP   AC
973'.04975 — dc20

The Iroquois Confederacy in Colonial New York

CANADA

NEW YORK

Lake Ontario

Lake Erie

MOHAWK

ONEIDA

ONONDAGA

CAYUGA

SENECA

Hudson River

PENNSYLVANIA

CREATION

The universe turned in the vastness of space
like a dream.
PETER BLUE CLOUD

Once, long ago in the Sky World, a woman was gathering seeds and berries when a great tree was uprooted, leaving a hole. Sky Woman fell through the hole and plunged down toward where there was no land. There was only water in which the fish and the animals swam. As Sky Woman fell, swans and geese flying over the water caught her with their wings.

"What shall we do with Sky Woman?" the birds asked. "She cannot fly like us, and she cannot swim. She needs a place to stand."

The creatures held a council and decided that they should dive into the sea and bring up some soil from the bottom. When they did, all failed except for muskrat. He was able to bring up a tiny bit of mud.

"But where shall we put it?" the animals wondered.

"On my back," turtle answered.

So the animals placed the bit of mud on turtle's back. It grew and grew until it became the earth. There, Sky Woman was set down. She dropped the seeds she had carried from the Sky World, and they grew into all of the plants and trees of the earth.

In this legend, the Sky Woman's children later became the Haudenosaunee.

5

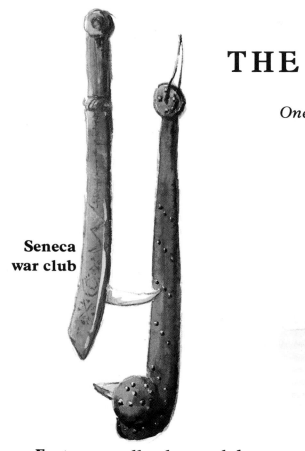

Seneca
war club

Eastern woodlands war club

longhouse

THE IROQUOIS LEAGUE

*One arrow is easily broken, but tied together,
no man can break the bundle.*

PEACEMAKER

The Haudenosaunee people were the Mohawk, Oneida, Onondaga, Cayuga, and Seneca tribes. They once occupied what is now the state of New York. Haudenosaunee means "those who build the longhouse" or "people of the longhouse," because they lived in long, rectangular houses. Their enemy, the Algonquin, may have given them the name Iroquois, meaning "bad or terrifying man." Or it may have come from another enemy tribe's word meaning "snake or real snake." The French adopted the name "Iroquois."

Long before the French and other white men came in the early 1600s, the Iroquois fought among themselves. But some time between the mid-1400s and early 1600s, a man called Peacemaker by some Iroquois, and Deganawidah by others, had a vision of all the people living happily together. This man may have

6

been of the Huron tribe, or a Mohawk, but he met Ayonwatha or Hiawatha, an Onondaga, who also wanted peace. The two men persuaded the tribes to work together and take up the path of peace. They asked them to form a confederacy or league, so that they could meet together to discuss issues that concerned all of them. Peacemaker uprooted a great white pine, and the warriors threw their weapons into the hole. The tree was replanted, and fifty chiefs linked hands around the trunk to hold it up if it fell. This act stood for the idea that all of the tribes together were stronger than when apart.

The Iroquois ceased fighting among themselves and helped each other in battles with enemy tribes.

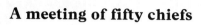
A meeting of fifty chiefs

The league was organized like the way people lived in a longhouse. Usually five families lived in a longhouse, with each family in a section with its own fire pit and hearth. In a similar fashion, all five tribes belonged to the league, but each had its separate place. The Mohawk became the "keepers of the Eastern Door," the Seneca the "keepers of the Western Door," the Onondaga, in the center of the territory, were "keepers of the Council Fire." In about 1723, the Tuscarora Indians of North Carolina joined the league after losing land to white settlers. The league now became the Six Nations.

The Iroquois confederate council came to be known as the Grand Council. It was made up of fifty chiefs. The council was divided into two bodies: the elder brothers, the Mohawk, Seneca, and Onondaga; the younger brothers, the Cayuga, Oneida, and Tuscarora. The names of the founders of the league are still used today. These leadership titles have been passed down through the Iroquois women.

In the early 1600s the Iroquois acquired guns from the Dutch. With the weapons, the league kept peace in their homelands. The league also controlled boat travel on the Great Lakes and the fur trade in Iroquois territory.

The notched staff was used by an Iroquois sachem to list the members of the great council.

M
O
H
A
W
K

O
N
E
I
D
A

O
N
O
N
D
A
G
A

C
A
Y
U
G
A

S
E
N
E
C
A

9

MEN

I am the string, the bow and the arrow.
MAURICE KENNY

blowgun

dart

Besides being powerful warriors, the Iroquois men were skilled hunters. On foot they silently stalked deer, or drove moose and caribou into the water where hunters in canoes killed them. The Iroquois hunters sometimes used a blowgun, a tube through which they blew darts with enough force to kill small creatures.

To lure game, the hunters made calls that sounded exactly like those of animals. Sometimes they disguised themselves with skins and lay in wait for their prey along trails or by water holes. Several men organized hunting parties to drive deer into fenced barriers, where they killed the animals with bows and arrows. The hunters only killed what they needed to survive.

The Iroquois liked to fish too. They used spears, bows and arrows, or lures and hooks to catch fish.

Iroquois men made all of their tools and weapons. They fashioned arrowheads from flint, jasper, or slate. They used springy wood, such as shagbark hickory, white ash, cedar, or white oak to make bows. They set round stones into wooden handles to make war clubs.

The trees in the forests also supplied wood for carving dishes. The men carved wooden bowls, ladles, and spoons. In addition, they built lightweight, swift canoes by fastening birch bark to wooden frames. They made the canoes waterproof by sealing the seams with a mixture of spruce gum and charcoal. And they used the wood of the forest and rawhide strips to make snowshoes for traveling in deep snow.

The Iroquois men wore deerskin shirts, leggings, breechcloths, and moccasins. Some of the men shaved their heads completely, leaving only a small amount of hair on top.

Iroquois spoons

lacrosse racket and ball

When Iroquois men weren't hunting, fishing, or working on crafts, they relaxed by playing games. One of their favorites was lacrosse, a game named by the French. Each player had a racket with which he caught and threw a ball made from a knot of wood. Trained teams of six to eight men attempted to hit the ball into goals set at the end of large fields or on the ice in the winter. A game was played from noon until evening and sometimes ended the following day. Teams from different tribes would compete on special days. The people who watched often placed bets on which team would win. The players carefully discussed plans for winning the game, which was fun as well as useful training for war.

FOOD

*For me it is of the utmost importance to touch earth,
the earth where the berries grow.*
MAURICE KENNY

husking pins

kernel scraper

mealing stone used
for grinding corn

The eastern woodland not only had plenty of game and fish, but it had fertile soil as well. Corn was so important to the Iroquois that they called it "our life." They held a festival when the seeds were planted, another when the young corn was green, and finally one for the harvest of the ripe ears. They planted squash and beans along with the corn. These vegetables were called the "three sisters," and their spirits protected the crops. Besides giving corn a special name, the Iroquois called squash "supporter of life" because it enriched their diet.

Food was roasted over fires in sunken pits or boiled in clay pots. Corn was eaten on the cob or in soup. The Iroquois ground corn and baked it into cakes.

13

making maple sugar

Sometimes they mixed cornmeal with maple sugar, dried berries, or chopped dried meat. They often boiled corn with wood ashes. This made it more nutritious and easier to remove the loosened hulls. The remaining corn became hominy. It was washed and boiled until tender. Hominy, corn, and beans were mixed together into succotash, a hearty dish that white settlers added to their diet.

Nuts and berries and other wild plants were also part of Iroquois meals. The wild strawberry, the earliest fruit of the year, was a special favorite. In the spring, the Iroquois held a festival to celebrate the feast of the ripe berries.

Spring was sugaring time. The Iroquois had a dance to bring warm weather so that the maple sap would flow. At the end of the sugaring, the Iroquois held a feast to celebrate.

WOMEN

Grandmothers go inside the longhouse.
They tend the fire, wait.
BETH BRANT

clan symbols

Women played an important part in Iroquois society. Iroquois heritage and inheritance were traced through them. Even though the members of the league council were men, the leadership was passed through the female line. If any member of the council misbehaved, the women had the power to remove him from office.

A woman was the head of a family. Every family belonged to a clan. Each clan, named after an animal, had a headwoman. Before the headwoman died or gave up her position, she carefully chose the female who would take her place. Her choice had to be approved by the clan's women, then the clan chiefs, and finally the league council.

beaded moccasins

bone awl

Although Iroquois men were responsible for clearing the fields, only women could plant the crops. The women sowed the seeds and tended the growing plants. They were in charge of the harvest that would keep the Iroquois from starving during the winter.

The women prepared all of the food for daily meals. They also dried or smoked it so that it would not spoil during the cold months. The food was stored in containers made from birch bark.

Iroquois mothers tanned hides, then used them to sew and decorate clothing and moccasins for their families. They sewed leather by punching holes in it with a bone awl, a pointed tool. Then they laced layers together with thread made from plant fibers. Their skirts and sleeveless dresses were fashioned from soft, tanned deerksins. Tougher tanned leather was made into leggings and soft-soled moccasins. The women decorated the clothing with porcupine quills.

burden frame

It was mounted on the woman's back and tied around her head with long straps. The extra rope at the top was used to tie in whatever was being carried.

Adult females made baskets for gathering roots and plants. They carried the baskets on their backs, fastened to a leather band around their foreheads. This tumpline was used to steady the pack and free the women's hands to carry other things.

Mothers and grandmothers used cedar bark, rushes, cornhusks, and cattails to weave mats and storage bags for the longhouse. Some women made coiled clay pots for cooking and storage.

Iroquois women had many tasks, but they also found time for games. Teams of women played a ball game in which a curved stick was used to toss and catch a buckskin ball filled with sand. The women also enjoyed a game called shinny. It was a little like hockey.

container made from corn husks

CHILDREN

Little baby, Little baby, Ride on Mother's back.
BETH BRANT

Onondaga cradleboard

corn-husk doll

Iroquois babies, from birth until they began to walk, spent much of their time in cradleboards. A cradleboard was made of a flat board with a footboard at the bottom and a bowed strip of wood at the top. This protected the baby's face. A leather covering held the baby in place. The mother tied the cradleboard to a strap around her forehead or shoulders when she carried her baby. She used the strap to hang the cradleboard on a limb or peg in the house. That way the baby was safe while the mother did her chores.

Girls cared for their younger brothers and sisters. If a girl had no little ones in her family, she took care of her baby cousins, whom she called brother or sister. Older girls went with the women to plant the seeds, weed the fields, and harvest the crops. Girls learned to cook by watching the women in the longhouse and by helping their mothers. When the women made clothes, they gave the girls small pieces of leather to sew into garments for their cornhusk dolls.

At about age six, Iroquois boys played with little bows and arrows and tiny blowguns. At first, a boy learned to hunt by playing at stalking birds and small game and by practicing with his miniature weapons. By age eight or nine, a boy was able to bring rabbits and birds home to his mother. Older boys formed hunting parties with others of their age. Often they took younger brothers or male cousins along. During his teens, a boy began hunting with the men, and his father became his teacher.

Iroquois children learned proper behavior by watching adults. They listened carefully to the stories told in the longhouses during the winter evenings. The stories taught them Iroquois history, customs, and values. If children were naughty, they were warned that a creature with a long nose would carry them off in a big pack basket.

SPIRITS AND HEALING

*We have been given the duty to live in harmony with
one another and other living things.*

FROM THE THANKSGIVING ADDRESS

False Face mask

turtle-shell rattle

**Onondaga ceremonial
water drum**

The Iroquois believed in Orenda, a powerful force that was present in all things. They saw Orenda working each day when the sun rose and when it set. The power was present in the budding spring, the growing corn, the falling leaves, and the snow of winter.

At times during the seasons, especially in the winter, evil spirits brought disease and illness to the village. Then a medicine man would perform a ceremony to drive away the unwanted spirits.

Each spring and fall, some Iroquois men joined a group called the False Face Society. They put on fierce-looking masks and traveled around the village to frighten away the evil spirits. All members of the society were men except for one woman who was the Keeper of the False Faces. The masks were of misshapen human faces carved from a living tree.

At the end of the eighteenth century, after the American Revolutionary War, the Iroquois had lost land to the Americans. They were poor because of the white settlers moving into their hunting grounds. The Iroquois League was no longer a powerful confederacy. Traditional customs were giving way to the white men's manner of living. A Seneca medicine man, Ganiodayo or Handsome Lake, had a vision. He was urged to tell the Iroquois to give up the new beliefs the white men had brought and not to drink alcohol. The directions in the vision became the Code of Handsome Lake and were called Gaiwiio or Good Word. The code described the proper way to marry, how to care for children and the aged, and how to live correctly from birth until death. Many Iroquois became followers of Handsome Lake.

WAMPUM

Wampum endows its carrier with a recognition of authority and truth.

FROM *KNOWLEDGE OF THE ELDERS*

Washington wampum belt

It recorded the treaty of peace between the U.S. government and the Iroquois while George Washington was president.

wampum belt

wampum strings

Wampum served many purposes among the Iroquois. The word comes from the Algonquins and means "white strings," because wampum was made from strings of white shell beads. The beads were strung into strands and woven into belts that were several feet long.

The Iroquois traded for wampum or received it as gifts from other tribes. They called the chiefs to council by sending wampum belts. A chief took the belt with him to be admitted into the council. Wampum belts were sent to another tribe with an invitation to join a war. Treaties between tribes and with the white men were recorded on belts made for the occasion.

The wampum belts became public records kept by the Onondaga. Several belts are still in existence and are prized Iroquois treasures, since they are a record of their history.

Europeans used wampum in place of coins, but the Iroquois never used wampum as money.

24

TODAY

House of five fires, they take you for a tomb,
but I know better.
ROBERTA HILL WHITEMAN

**Joseph Brant, a Mohawk war leader
who fought against the Americans
during the Revolutionary War**

General John Sullivan

The Iroquois men were fearless warriors, and the league united them into a powerful force. During the French and Indian War from 1754 to 1763, the Iroquois sided with the British. But, during the American Revolutionary War, 1775–1781, the Iroquois were divided. The league broke up when all but the Oneida and Tuscarora sided with the British. In 1779, General John Sullivan, under George Washington's orders, destroyed the villages of the Iroquois who had helped the British.

After the war, white men wanted to settle on Iroquois land. So the new United States government forced the Iroquois to move. Most of the Cayuga and Mohawk were sent to reservations, land set aside by the government for Native Americans, in Canada. The Oneida, even though they had helped the U.S. government, were sent to a reservation in Wisconsin. A few Senecas went to Pennsylvania and Oklahoma. The remaining Senecas, Tuscaroras, and Onondagas were placed on reservations in New York State.

modern longhouse

Today the Oneida have a reservation in Green Bay, Wisconsin. The Oneida Nation Museum displays a reconstructed village with a longhouse.

Brantford, Ontario, is named for Joseph Brant. It is the site of the Woodland Indian Cultural Education Center, where one can do research on Iroquois culture and history and see modern arts and crafts.

The Six Nations Grand River Indian Reserve in Ontario is home to thousands of Iroquois, mostly Mohawks and Cayugas.

At Niagara Falls, New York, there is the Turtle Native American Center for the Living Arts. It is a museum, art gallery, and craft shop operated by the Iroquois.

Iroquois children go to schools on the reservations as well as in cities and towns where their parents live and work. Some Iroquois are farmers and mechanics. Mohawk steel-construction workers have helped build high bridges, towers, and many of New York City's skyscrapers.

Other Iroquois go to college and become teachers, doctors, lawyers, engineers, and businessmen. There are Iroquois artists, writers, and musicians who keep their heritage alive through their art.

The ancient festivals are still celebrated, and lacrosse is a competitive sport among Indians and non-Indians.

Women continue to head traditional clans, and the Iroquois League continues to meet in a Grand Council.

MY FEET ARE ELMS

My feet are elms, roots in the earth
my heart is the hawk
my thought the arrow that rides
   the wind across the valley
my spirit eats with eagles on the mountain crag
   and clashes with the thunder
my grass is the breath of my flesh
   and the deer is the bone of my child
my toes dance on the drum
   in the light of the eyes of the old turtle

MAURICE KENNY

decorated peace pipe

I LIE IN GRANDMOTHER'S BED

I lie in Grandmother's bed
and dream the earth into a turtle.
She carries us slowly across the universe.
The sun warms us.
At night the stars do tricks.
The moon caresses us.

BETH BRANT

AUTHOR'S NOTE

The Thanksgiving Address mentioned after the quote on page 21 is a long prayerful speech that dates back to the founding of the Iroquois Confederacy. It is said at the opening and closing of council meetings.

The Hiawatha of the Iroquois is not the Hiawatha of Longfellow's legend.

INDEX